· POETRY THAT HEALS BROKENNESS·

stretching the spirit

D1444064

REGENIA WILKERSON

Regenia Wilkerson
P.O. Box 1842, Cadiz, KY 42211
RegeniaSP@gmail.com

Back cover author photo taken by Franklin Clark
Cover design by Yvonne Parks at www.pearcreative.ca
Interior design by Katherine Lloyd at TheDESK
Publishing coordination by www.hitthemarkpublishing.com

Printed in the United States of America

stretching
the
spirit

DEDICATION

I dedicate this book to my family, specifically to my mother, Emmie B. Wilkerson, sisters Rosie Cox and Patricia Dawson, brothers Milton and Anthony Wilkerson; my true friends and my church family at New Life Ministries in Hopkinsville, Kentucky; Senior Pastors Will and Mary Holland and Pastor William Holland who stuck by me during the trying times in my life. I love all of you! I also want to extend this dedication to include anyone who is struggling with divorce, unemployment, low self-esteem or any of life's problems. Don't give up. Help is on the way. Just keep trusting in the Lord Jesus Christ and He will restore you.

ENDORSEMENTS

*A*fter a lifetime of dedicated public service to Kentucky's families and children, Regenia Wilkerson now voices the source of her strength through the words of her poetry. Throughout her personal and professional life, Regenia's moral compass and values have directed her as she has toiled for over twenty-five years in the juvenile justice system, enriching and inspiring the lives of those that she has met and served. Her poetry reflects her strength, her love and the dedication that Regenia personifies.

—Susan Stokely Clary
Court Administrator, Court Clerk and General Counselor
for the Supreme Court of Kentucky and
Co-author of the book, *Kentucky Juvenile Law*

*B*ecause the Bible is written in verse, there is no better way to express the Word of God than through the stanzas of poetry. Poetry is a major key to enhancing relationships, which the Lord God, Himself, loves to share by conversing deeply with His chosen people.

Relationships are God-given opportunities to share one's inner being with another, creating a bond of unity. This bond of unity can break the walls of any barrier, such as race, creed, sex, or even religion. When the walls of any barrier are broken, then the relationship can grow into a rich cultural environment that will allow the truth to be realized, understood, and appreciated by all. The powerful and influential poetry in this book is capable of causing joy to be produced between a man and a woman, peace to escalate between two nations, or an unfathomable love to mature between the church and the one true God.

In the Name of the Lord Jesus Christ,

—William J. Holland, Pastor
New Life Ministries

ACKNOWLEDGEMENTS

I would like to thank VFW Post 7890 and the Ladies Auxiliary of Post 7890 in Cadiz, Kentucky, for their support and encouragement while I was writing this book. Also, I want to thank Edrena Harrison for her support and encouragement. Thanks to Betty, Carolyn, Charletta, Christy, Geri, Janie O, Jerry, Mildred G, Rosetta, Rosa, Shonnon, Susie, and Tim.

CONTENTS

It's Deep

(The Love of God)

The love of God is alive,
A never ending river with an undercurrent
that flows on and on and on…
It's like a refreshing breeze or drink that soothes,
the tiredness of your spirit and soul,
On a hot summer's day, It's deep the love of God
Deeper than the deepest mountain, valley or cliff,
Deeper than the carnal mind can grasp
The love of God
It's a rhapsody of ions; it's a rhapsody of color,
the anointing,
A convergence of spirit, soul and body,
It's the oneness, the unity with God, it's pure light
It's deep the love of God

"It's Deep" was written on a cold winter's night. I attended a Wednesday night service at my church called One Hour of Power with Pastor William Holland. During the services

while he was preaching, he laid his hands on my head and prayed. After retiring to bed, I was awakened by a strong desire to write and words began to just flow like a river from deep within my being. I grabbed a pen and paper and started writing. This would be the beginning of a journey which would stir up my gifts.

Life

Is a circle filled with curves, valley mountain tops,
slopes, gorges and bumps,
Life is cycle, a range of low, slows and
spins, starts and stops.
Life is a highway filled with high and low roads, cross-
ings, passages, pathways as well as freeways.
Life is a destination filled with decisions: right or left,
wrong or right, good or bad, maybe, maybe nots,
happy or sad.

Life is being stuck
Smack dab
In the middle
"Life offers choices"

*"Life" was written when I was reflecting on how I felt at
that particular stage in my life. I felt like I had been in a
washing machine and was going through every phase of
the cleansing cycle of life. It just felt good to write it down
and to meditate on my thoughts.*

Life

(AKA Existence)

To have depth
To matter and to be matter
To exist beyond the horizon
To breath
To stand
To stead
To reign
To be in the rain, even on a plain
To be accounted for
Like one in a band, marching,
A soldier, a pilgrim
Planning to land on foreign soil,
To toil, to be in a mix
A big abyss, a matrix
"Called Life"

"Life (AKA Existence)" talks about knowing that you matter, that your life has purpose, and knowing that your

Life

existence means something. Realize that life isn't easy but make the best of it whether you are a soldier, a pilgrim on foreign soil or a plain. It is like a big abyss, but stand and be responsible. Life can be like a tossed salad mix at times.

Loneliness Brings Praise

I must embrace it like;
I embrace a friend with a hug,
I must enjoy it like a slug of an almond joy,
Loneliness
It is a state of being that takes me far beyond
my comfort zone
Into another dimension
Where fear cannot grip, strip, trip or hold me in de-
spair,
Even if, it is not fair
Loneliness
A solitary, thing an unfrequented, unwanted,
unknown companion,
A loathsome thing, with a sting,
It makes me want to sing,
To do the thing that brings unthinkable joy:
Praise, Praise, Praise…
The only thing that phases out its sting.

Loneliness is a state of being and in order to overcome it, you must treat it like a friend who you would embrace. Learn to be joyous and content even in the face of adversity. The sting of loneliness is diminished by praising and acceptance.

Faith

Faith is trust
Faith is hope
Faith is strength
Faith gives and receives
Faith is love
Faith cares
Faith is substance
Faith is evidence
Faith is confidence
Faith is unseen
Faith believes
Faith is loyalty
Faith is principles
Faith is an allegiance
Faith is a link
Faith is taking action;
Faith is now!!!

Faith

It takes faith to do anything because faith is taking action in the now. Now signifies domination of time. Faith is an allegiance and involves principles and trust and expectation.

Entanglement Breeds Entanglement

Be not entangled
Or
Ensnared
Trapped, Lured,
Restricted, Limited
Embroiled
Or
Caught in bondage
Enslaved, barred, fenced in,
In a stronghold,
Entangled breeds Entanglement

A former pastor and family friend, Reverend J. T. Bacon, used to say, "Get mixed up but not tangled up." He was referring to associations with people and the cares of the world. I have always remembered what he said because he was like a spiritual father to us. He and his wife, Mrs. Ruth, were the first folks that I told about getting saved

besides my family and the people at Little River Baptist Church in Caledonia , Kentucky. Our pastor, Reverend RV Gunn, had a stroke and Reverend Bacon became our pastor and he baptized me on a cold October day in a pond down from the church on the Wharton property.

Tomorrow

Is a future reference word that can only be,
Visualized
Counted on,
Expected to happen,
Hoped for,
Not seen, like faith,
Tomorrow follows today,
The morning after,
The storms,
The trials,
The tribulation,

The highs,
The lows,
The hurts,
The failures,
And
The disappointments in our lives,
All hinges on **Tomorrows,**
Tomorrows are not promised,
"Live for Today"

Tomorrow

We all make plans for tomorrow not knowing if we will be around for today. We look forward to tomorrow because it brings us closer to our breakthrough. And we are hopeful that time will heal our wounds and extinguish our hurts. The thoughts that reality is "now" and today is the time to live echoed through my mind as I penned this poem.

Spiritual Stretching

Is giving when you have nothing left to give
Smiling when your heart is broken into pieces
Going the extra mile by praising when
you don't have the energy
Admitting to failure when you know
that you are wrong
Apologizing when you know that you are right

Spiritual Stretching
Is expecting victory in the face of adversity
Giving beyond your means, until it hurts
Requires a testing of your faith, which worketh patience
Walking situations out, only to realize you were being
carried by God
It is spiritual growth
Not wondering what would Jesus do? Just doing it,
instead of displaying it,
Running a good race
Fighting a good fight
Like a competitive boxing match to see
the end results
Being Jesus to others

Spiritual Stretching
Is allowing Jesus total access to us and us to Him
It is spiritual agreement
Quantum leaping from the natural
to the supernatural realm
A combination of the former and latter rain knowing
that God transcends time

Spiritual Stretching
Involved movement and action;
Standing, kneeling, dancing, praising, vocalizing, obe-
dience and self – denial,
Spiritual stretching is: flexing your spiritual muscles to
complete kingdom work,
Building up holy perfected praise
which is acceptable to God

"Spiritual Stretching" is a phrase I coined to describe how one should exercise spiritual muscles as well as physical muscles. It is applying spiritual knowledge to situations in our lives, which then brings about growth and change in our spiritual man. I am learning to expect victory in the good and bad times and to never give up but to put my hope and trust in Jesus.

What Is It?

Oh! How it flows, Oh! How it falls, soothes, cleanses,
And it lubricates like smearing oil,
It is visual, tangible, vibrant, rejuvenating,
A restorer, a bondage yoke breaking repellent,
For good or evil, ridding the Spirit of dirt and grime,
Brightening one's aura,
Calming both natural and supernatural storms
in our lives,
The genuine, inspiring, revealing, euphoric, illuminat-
ing
Tranquil presence of God, What is it?
Oh! "The Anointing"

"What Is It?" talks about the power of the anointing and the presence of God in our lives. The anointing breaks bondages and restores, it soothes and calms. It acts like a lubricant or cleanser that is applied to cleanse the spirit.

The Substitute

He took your place on an old rugged cross,
Died the death of a sinner,
Took on all of our wrongs to make things right,
He does not complain about rising early
and toiling all night,
Like normal laborers, teachers,
doctors or social workers,
He is a 24-7 type of guy, always ready
and able to see you through,
Whether in the courtroom, a sickroom
or on the battlefield,
So no weapon formed against you will prosper,
He hung high and stretched wide for you and for me,
He became the propitiation for our sins,
Whose blood covered and reconciled all of our sins,
yeah, the whole world.

*"The Substitute" was written in five minutes or less while
I was in bed. I heard my sister Pat talking about the per-
ils and rewards of substitute teaching and teaching in*

general. Teachers are over-worked and underpaid. They rise early and spend countless hours after school grading papers, attending meetings and taking classes to further their education. I began to think about how Jesus was our "Substitute"; He went to the cross and died the death of a sinner just for you and for me.

Building a Bridge

Our faith builds a bridge,
Along with Christ replacing what was broken in Eden,
By passing our stepping stone of unbelief,
Hindrances to our faith,
These enemies of our faith,
Continually suppress our understanding;
Of what it means to be a new creature in Christ,
The newness and freshness of being a believer,

The

Cleansing of our sins, being reborn;

And

Not knowing our place in the body of Christ,
This should not be, for we are the sons of God;
He has covered our sins with His blood,
We can come into His presence without guilt or shame,

For

We are your righteousness in Christ Jesus,
Logos who make the word work for us,
Through the confession of our faith,

Now

Walking epistles;
Billboards for Christ Jesus

Building a Bridge

Connecting ourselves with God builds a bridge to help us get around or over obstacles in our paths or in our lives. Belief requires faith and faith builds the structure, a relationship of trust that can block hindrances that keep us bound to unbelief and brokenness.

Love is Timeless

Love is faith
Love is unrestricted
Love is free
Love is not selfish
Love is caring
Love is giving
Love is kind
Love has no boundaries
Love is intense
Love is togetherness
Love is enthusiastic
Love is adoration
Love is favor
Love is timeless
Love is Jesus

Love is truly timeless and I was thinking about what love really means to me. Love encompasses so many things such as faith, time, giving, caring, adoration, favor and kindness. Then, I remembered that is what Jesus represents—love. He is the reason we can express love.

My Open Heart

My heart is more than a chambered colossal network,
It holds the key to the seasons of my life,
I've experienced some winters,
Where life appeared to be a series of dead dreams, mis-
ery, bareness, coldness and stillness,
In the cavities of my heart,
Then comes spring, a time to spring forward,
Into newness of life,
Only to find that I'm still at a crossroad,
Between the summers and winters of my life,
Summer, a fruitful time of fulfillment,
happiness and beauty,
The time to enjoy family, holiday festivities
and even weddings,
A time to be free and joyful in one's heart,
Fall, my heart reflects on the former seasons,
I come to realize who I am and where I need to go,
I will keep my heart open,
Allowing, God to complete His work in me,

I won't let my heart become stony,
With the cares of this world,

My Open Heart

No, I won't let them take control of my heart,
I will be strong, like a flint;
Releasing the cares and the contents of my heart,
To the Lord thus,
bringing unlimited satisfaction to my heart,
Oh! If, you could see into my open heart,
Then you would know that it has been seasoned with
God's love and grace

My healing from hurt and rejection came out in this poem. Life has seasons and we will experience something different in each phase of our lives. "My Open Heart" is about discovering one's self and how to find the real you. It requires some soul searching, prayer, and some alone time with the Father. We must learn to release the contents of our hearts to the Lord and find satisfaction in knowing His grace and mercies that He extends are new each day. Just remain open and know that He cares deeply for us.

Mending My Brokenness

God is mending my brokenness piece by piece,
As a Seamstress mends a garment or the way
an Artist mends a torn canvas,
Skillfully and with care because,
I am fearfully and wonderfully made,
He uses the hands of a carpenter,
putting the pieces together,
According to the pattern, He has carved from
His spoken Word,
He uses His all seeing eyes, which are magnificent
and as accurate as the eagle eye
He sprinkles His wisdom which is endless
into my being,
Making sure to erase the pain and restore
everything to its original state,
Before the breaches occurred
in the pinnacle of my being,
You know that God has a storeroom in heaven,
Filled with replacement parts only He can order,
He is a Specialist and He specializes in the impossible,
Let him repair you!

Sometimes we need to be repaired or rebuilt. I went through a time of brokenness. However, I felt the hand of God moving in my life and I found peace as I searched for it. He continues to erase my pain as I press forward, leaving the past behind and as I surrender to His will and purpose for my life. Never look back if a relationship did not work before. The likelihood of it working again is small. I did not say impossible, for all things are possible with God. Remember God closes and opens doors in our lives for a reason. He will reveal the reason in His time, not ours.

Our Love

Our Love is one of a kind; it has defied all odds,
Just when we had thrown the towel in
and declared it's over,
A flame ignited within our spirits,
That refreshed and reconnected two hearts
that once beat as one,
Reuniting an unquenchable union,
orchestrated by the hands of God,
Our separation proved what we always knew
that our love,
Remain timeless, forgiving and forever true,
Reminding us what God truly joins together
no man can put asunder,
And on this our "Wedding Day"
we want to share with you,
The story of a lifetime,
Filled with our past, present
and future hopes and aspirations,
A togetherness that proves
love is the greatest gift of all

"Our Love" was born from an idea my friend Charletta had for her cousin Beverly's wedding. Beverly was going to remarry her high school sweetheart and ex-husband Ben Watkins. They were to be remarried on February 18, 2012. When I was asked to write a poem for them, I told Charletta that I would have to pray about it and that God would have to give me the words. I explained to her that I just could not write without a word from the Lord. The following Monday, I was driving to work and the Lord began to give me words for this poem. I said, "Lord can you hold those thoughts until I get to the parking lot or somewhere that I can write?" I'm so glad that He gave me this poem to share with them, their children, their grand-children, family and their guests, because Ben went home to be with the Lord four months after they were reunited in holy matrimony.

Love from Afar

I have loved you from afar,
Now, I want to love you, close up and personal,
With the love only God can put in one's heart,
A love that is real, vibrant and long lasting,
Not a worldly carnal sadistic lustful emotion,
I want to be in tune and focused on
every beat of your heart,
In perfect rhythm, in timing with your spirit,
And at the heart of every decision you make in life,
How else can two walk together unless they agree?
I want to be one with you as; I am one with Christ,
Who has repaired the breeches in my heart,
So, I can love again the way God ordained love,
From the beginning of time,
The time is right and the season is here,
For me to love again and God has chosen you,
I am the missing rib that he took from your side,
The one that my spirit has been waiting for patiently,
I will cherish this God given love for a life time,
"I love you"

When I wrote this poem, I was thinking about how Adam must have felt when he finally saw his helpmate. He was lonely, for there was no suitable mate found for him. Every creature had a mate except Adam who was graciously naming them all. I believe I will be glad when the "guy" finds me. I will treat him according to his position as the head in the marriage. The Bible states that a man who finds a wife finds a good thing. I believe that he will recognize me and I will recognize him because Jesus must reside in our temples. There is a season and time for everything and it is all about timing and destiny. I think it is one of my best poems. It was definitely written for a man who can be the prince and king in his home and treat the "girl" according to her position as the weaker vessel in marriage.

What the Cross Means to Me

The cross is an emblem,
a symbol of suffering and shame,
A crucifix, where Christ was affixed,
A place for the condemned to hang and to die,
He took my place and paid my bond,
Jesus laid down his life and died,
For me,
An unworthy sacrificial exchange,
Therefore;
The cross represents a junction, an intersection,
Where the spiritual winds and directions converge,
Northward, Southward, Eastward and Westward,
At a crossroad, a decisive mark,
Pointing the way,
Forward,
To
Secure the prize,
Eternal Life

I can never repay Christ for what He did for me by going to the cross to pay a debt for me. I strive to be more like Him each day, but I often miss the mark and fall short of His glory. This poem reminds us of Christ's awesomeness and His love for us. The cross represents an intersection, a decisive mark. We can go forward or backward, go back to our past or press toward our future to receive the gift of eternal life. Believe it or not, our past can affect our future.

The Tomb Dream

I dreamed that I was there with you…
When, you were placed in Joseph's tomb,
I was transported back through the ages of time,
To see the sacrifice that you made for me
and for others,
I know that you were falsely accused and lied on,
Spit on
Slapped
Stabbed
Mocked
Crowned with thorns
Walked and carried a cross
Lots were cast for your tunic
Nails were hammered into your hands and feet,
These things you endured as the Sacrificial Lamb,
Slain from the foundation of the world,
I hovered above in the tomb, as your body,
Laid silent and still, in the heart of the earth,
Three days and three nights,
While your spirit was busy, setting Patriarchs,
Abraham, Isaac and Jacob and others free,

You took back the keys of life and death,
Stripping Satan and his cohorts of their powers

Amazingly, your spirit returned
and you spoke with authority,
Flexed your resurrection muscles and said
"Death can't keep me down,"
Then, you shook free of your grave clothes,
as a spiritual explosion occurred,
You neatly folded your grave clothes indicating
that you would be back
Defeating death and the grave, rising with "all power,"
In those beautiful nail-scarred hands,
I woke up in my bed awestruck,
No longer wondering what happened in the tomb,
Jesus
"Now," I am a "Believer"

I really dreamed about the tomb experience and it was an awesome dream. I'm glad that I was allowed to remember so much detail. Jesus paid the price, a ransom with His life. This dream really helped me to explain the death and resurrection to my Vacation Bible Class that I taught and it was so much fun. My students were the best!

It Was Your Promises

You who knew me when,
I was far off,
You, who told me to go forth only as a twinkle
in my Dad's eyes,
Later becoming a seed, a being
in the receptacle of my mother's womb,
It was you, who named me;
as I was birthed into this old sinful world,
It was you, who placed me in the care
of two earthly beings,
To guide me and teach me about life and your ways,
It was you, who called out to me
to repent and to be born again,
It was you, who once again placed me
into another receptacle,
The womb called the "Church"
It was you Jesus, who made me one of your brides,
To help fulfill the promise that you would come back,
For a church without spot or wrinkle,
It was you, who promised to never leave or forsake me,
You said that you would be with me
even to the end of the ages

It was and still is your promises which are keeping me
faithful and alive,

For your promises are true,
Thank you for being "You"

*God's promises are true because He is faithful and we should
always thank Him for His love and kindness towards us.
He is always looking out for us and gives us free will to
accept His promises or to reject them. The Word keeps His
word. It is all written in the Holy Bible.*

Words

Are used to communicate,
Expressions through writing, speaking or singing,
Spoken eloquently,
Calmingly or irritatingly,
Words are remarks, phrases, comments or commands,
They can surprise, hurt or calm us,
Affirm us,
Build us up,
Or tear us down,
Words can bring life or death
depending on how they are perceived,
Not to bring destruction, sadness or despair,
Use them wisely to express joy, kindness or happiness,
Use them to build,
Friendships and Relationships,
Godly promises based on faith, hope and truth

How many times have we said, "I wish that I had never said a word"? Words are important because we use them to communicate and they can create life or death. We should

strive to say positive things and say things in a construc-tive manner to avoid tearing down individuals as well as ourselves. We should always try to think before we speak. Remember, Christ spoke things into the atmosphere and they happened. He gave His believers the same authority; we just don't know how to use the gifts He blessed us with. We need more wisdom and understanding.

In Your Presence

I'm overwhelmed by your presence,
The way you speak to me,
Look at me,
And the way you touch my spirit,
I feel like a Queen in your presence,
In the presence of a King, there is fullness of joy…
You literally take my breath away
with your sweet words and affections,
I hear you calling me and my heart skips a beat,
To the rhythm of praise
from your throne room of grace,
The twinkles in your eyes draw me deeper
into the realm where you dwell,
Into your courts where mercy and praise run rampant,
I am caught up in the flow of the anointing,
Where time has no control,
Hours of glorious throne room praise,
Wisdom, knowledge and understanding
are my portions,
Worship that raises the roof within my soul,
A spiritual explosion with you and me in the midst,
It is overwhelming

There is fullness of joy in the presence of the Lord and I do feel like a queen when I worship Him because I am surrounded by His love. I feel special when He talks to me, surprises me with things that I have desired, or answers questions that I have pondered over in my heart. He is my King and I feel like Esther when I enter into His courts with thanksgiving and praise. I realize that this is what being in His presence is all about; it is a special alone time with someone who loves you and you love them too. This could apply to a relationship with that special someone too. You know, it doesn't hurt to have a name that means queen or queenly (Regenia).

A Lonely Place

I've been in a wilderness, a desert barren lonely place,
A state of chaos,
To answer to a higher calling from above,
I've learned to face some difficult truths about myself,
I've gone through some spiritual struggles,
some great battles,
And I suffered some mammoth losses,
And
I toiled, but like the Lily, a flower neither labors or toils,
What a revelation,
Then, I realized that you were with me,
My champion, my Lord cheering me on,
I must go through,
And contend for my faith,
Worrying not about strength but endurance,
To
Run the race with patience,
Knowing that when I am weak,
You show yourself to be mighty and strong,
I have found pleasure in this desert place,
Your grace, mercy, peace and assurance,
Now rest upon me

Sometimes we have to go to that lonely place to find ourselves and to discover that we are never alone when we have God in our lives. Trials come our way sometimes to make us strong and to cause us to be still so we can hear from God. We must fight for our faith and be content where we are and be still and let the Lord fight our battles and supply our needs. The lily does not toil or spin. It has no worries, nor should we. I added the lily section because Senior Pastor Mary Holland loves lilies. They are her favorite flowers.

I See Jesus

I see Jesus when, I look into the face of all of his people,
I see Jesus when, I gaze upon creation
and see its beauty…
I see Jesus as I look upward into the sky,
And fix my sights on the kaleidoscopic colors,
And hues of the covenant reminding rainbow,
I see and feel Jesus as I, stand in the midst,
Of the winds of change that blow all around
and about me,
For, I am his image mirrored,
A, living and breathing reflection of "Him."

I knew that this poem was spiritually inspired when I had to look up how to spell kaleidoscopic. I just don't use those kinds of words. I do know that Jesus loves all kinds of people and He wants us to follow His example of how to love and respect each other. We should reflect His image as we go about our daily affairs. You might be the only Jesus someone sees during the day. His presence is evident in the beauty of his creations. Just think about a fall outdoor

scene of beautiful trees that have been kissed by the frost or the beautiful colors of the rainbow. The rainbow is a reminder of God's promise never to destroy Earth with water again. When I see it in the sky, I am reminded of His unmerited favor, grace and His mercies which are new each day, and I am so grateful.

My Wounded Heart

My heart has been wounded,
The wounds in my heart are there,
because of the tentacles of demonic forces,
That comes against my spirit such as unfruitful
relationships, anger, greed, jealousy, backbiting, worry,
uncertainty, passivity, unbelief and poverty,
They are very prevalent to the cares of life,
Although, these things oppress me,
I am keeping my wounded heart open…
Open to give and receive love to face challenges ahead,
And to go through doors that the Lord
has opened as a way of escape,
I will not fear,
my wounds are covered with the smearing ointment,
Of the Anointed One – Jesus,
He has made my wounds visible yet, painless,
As a testimony of where I came from
to where I am today,
A wounded vessel, not ashamed to be
viewed, touched or handled,
A vessel of honor now filled with God's mercy
and grace

"My Wounded Heart" is a sequel to "My Open Heart." My trials have made me stronger and I am not ashamed of the difficulties and failed relationships in my life. Yes, I went through some pain. But no pain and no gain. I gained much more than I lost. My wounds will help someone else who is hurting and who needs to know that they are not alone. Time does bring healing and you can look back and say, "I was on the wrong path. I hope that those who were on it with me will find the path that is right for them and stop going in circles and being bound to circumstances that only they can change by letting go of anger, hatred, and self-pity." Just shut the doors to the past, move on, let go and let God. Stop being limited.

Made in the USA
Lexington, KY
25 May 2013